AF397518

A smile with a tear

102 poems by Lawrence Gelmon

© Lawrence Gelmon 2018

Publisher: BoD - Books on Demand, Stockholm, Sweden

Printer: BoD - Books on Demand, Norderstedt, Germany

ISBN: 978-91-7699-693-5

To my parents

1. Feet

When the mist eases

I see you over there

in your white suit

How many times

have I thought

I will walk over

make love to her

fertilize her

give her my manhood

But my feet are stiff

I can't get loose

I look and look

I remain standing

How you were

I may never know

2. Room

It was when the flowers reaches their peak

when the days were long

the nights were balmy cool

and you were the most beautiful of all

We went all along the path

to get near to the ocean

which we both loved

as we loved each other

You said I could take you

to the end of the world

But I only wanted to take you

to my room.

3. The Plug

My scars are also yours

when I suffer

you feel as well

We live together

forever

as we said that time

so long ago

But my days are numbered

soon you are alone

Pull out the plug

so I'll sail away

4. The Couch

My new shoes shine in the dark

The brand is good

The fit is perfect

But they still remind me

of a failure

I don't want to run

I don't want to jog

I don't want to walk

I want to sit here in the couch

munching and munching

junk after junk

burp and fart

zap and zip

What a man I am.

5. Harp

If you were a harp

I would stroke the strings

as if they were of velvet

I would listen

to every tone

as if it were my own

In major and minor

yes, in every tone

I would love you.

6. Feet 2

You feet are so big

I can stand on them

for I'm so small

I can tramp and tramp

and you stand steady

You look down on me

ruffle my hair

and smile.

7. Home

The shadows of the trees

scare me

The wind which whispers

go away

make me tremble

The owl breaks the silence

a friend in the forest

is what I need

The steps get straighter

the speed gets quicker

I have found my strength

to take me home.

8. Whisky

Many years have passed

and often I have thought of you

most of all in spring

when the buds are comimg out

Our meetings in the seventies

when our bodies ached

after tenderness and caressing

You gave and you got

and seemed so happy

But one day the letter came

when it was all over

I tried to be a man

and took a whisky.

9. Cuddle

The frog jumps joyfully

ahead in the wet grass

Is it for fun

or

is he hunting

after food for today

Why don't I jump

when I feel joie de vivre

Why am I cool

When I want to cuddle.

10. Faraway

When the ground gives away

beneath our feet

When the friends

turn aside

When the church bells

ring wrong signals

When the women

smack their lips

Then it's time

to get away

to buy a one-way ticket

Not too near

but far faraway.

11. Anna

Like a shooting star

you slide down the hill

Naturally and elegant

you shine in the ski slope

That almost always

have a comfortable margin

is not only luck

You are a queen in the tracks

but even beyond

You support the wild animals

but who is the tigress

Well, it's you.

12. The Mead

You're gazing over there

What are you looking for my friend

Is it the meads billowing greenness

The horizons deep blue

or do you turn around

to the memory

you want to awaken

When the horses were grazing

When the skies were a deeper blue

and the girl you loved

who you could love

was with you

But not anymore.

13. The Darkness

A walk in the dark

alone in the forest

sounds from birds

was it a cuckoo

it was an owl

A shadow over the path

I get scared

it was from a swaying branch

I giggle over my fear

I'm not a piece of folly

but a man

with stature personality

But in the evening

in the great wilderness

we are all small.

14. Ideas

All my thoughts

disappear in cosmos

they want out

If they stay

I will go mad

A mess

of ideas

fighting together

Noone win

They are all

beaten

and I

start climbing

on the wall.

15. Buds

In spring it is common

to scrutinize the buds up closely

they are keen to grow

become big and strong

arouse our admiration

To see but not to touch

to take delight in their nature

not in a vase on the terrace

Ring bell ring

It's time for the buds to burst.

16. Espresso

A breath

between our kisses

feels like an eternity

I must taste you

every second

A gleam of espresso

lingers on

It excites me

and it excites you

to be enchanted

I give you my taste

it's not espresso.

17. Propose

A sensation

is something surprising

and big

Just as when

I proposed to you

a little bit for fun

I didn't really dare

but you said yes

I who have the gift of speech

got totally dumb

Does she honestly want me

a man like me

who really is not

a husband, father or soldier

Where is the world going.

18. Death

Death is my friend

the only one I have

My mother is dead

My father is dead

My wives have run away

I have no children

My brother took an overdose

My neighboors are eskimoes

I count the days

until old Nick takes me

and I

get rid of

my humiliation.

19. Home ground

The moon passes into clouds

so even the sun

What can I do

other than cry

over all the games

I have lost

on away grounds

On home grounds

I'm unbeaten

and very much acclaimed

by all the virgins.

20. Love

You just left

when the money dried up

when the champagne didn't taste

when the jewels were pawned

But my heart was big

there was room for you

although you are a fortune-hunter

I will never forget your laugh

your bright blue eyes

you skills in love-making

You are etched in my mind.

21. Dare

One morning

I thought

all is new

noone knows what will happen

least of all me

What can I do

as I usually do

or as I dream

Shall I dare.

22. Ghost

To all its extent

she doesn't understand him

His gloomy soul

is a vacuum

for an explorer

She has never

travelled beyond the horizon

not even in her dreams

She understands that she

can never see him

other than a ghost.

23. Curiosity

To gaze towards the field

and remember childhoods

delightful laughter

when we were playing

We were young then

and didn't know anything

about the years to come

When all is repeated

in a circle

and kills curiosity

about gifts of life

Yes, then we were young.

24. Shadow

Through the venetian blinds

a ray of light

Is it morning

There is hope

I have survived

the nights torments

A woman's shadow

I see in the corner of my eye

She's prances by slowly.

25. The cat

The world is going to pieces

and we as well

But is it so

Some are shot there

and lava spurts out there

But my mother in the country

is safe

in her sheltered spot

with the siamese.

26. Fuck

Fuck fuck fuck

not off

not you

but Love Love Love

the whole summer

until you meet

someone you love

Then it will be couple-fuck

until you get tired

then it is

fuck fuck fuck

as a single

Till you meet someone

you love.

27. The melody

You are humming

our song

from the summer of 69

We were young then

we didn't know anything else

than our love

Year after year

has shaped us

for better and for worse

But that melody

is still us.

28. Trolls

Alone we walk through the forest

but I'm not afraid

I can rest in your arms

if we stay for a while

Then I take courage

and we can go on

among dwarves and trolls

they feel now as my friends

Come play with me

we play dancing music

on the small plot of grass.

29. Distance

The distance between us

was not miles or inches

only just words

that did not depend upon

that you being woman and I a man

but our languages

You were Grecian

without English

I was a Scandinavian

without Greek

But your curly smile

and your nipples under the blouse

gave a promise

which words can not.

30. If

If the sun goes into clouds

I'll take away the clouds

If your tire has no air

I'll use my lungs

If the rats eat up the food

I'll shoot a bullock

If your neighboor play loudly

I'll dance until midnight

Whatever happens

I'm there

with you.

31. The seagull

The seagull travels through the clouds

How did I get here

so high above all

Am I brave

thinks the seagull

when an airplane flies by

Am I ambitious

thinks the seagull

gazing at the sun

I could fix it

I have a goal

I can't miss

How faraway can it be.

32. The path

The path I'm walking

has no end

I wear out my soles

my calves are aching

my stomach is rumbling

for my food is all gone

I throw away the rucksack

to lighten the burden

But you walk with ease

an elf by my side

you are beaming with energy

How will it ends.

33. Away

You're treading on your path

but are getting nowhere

you cykling on your road

but are getting nowhere

You have no goal

which is written in the stars

Where do you want to go

Away away away

Where do you want to live

There there there

Follow your inner voice

Yes yes yes.

34. Nothing

Who is the mother of the sun

asked a child

What do I know

and started thinking

I don't know

how to do anything

and if I say something

you won't understand anything

I am doomed

to wander alone

introvert and unreachable

among all others

who don't know anything.

35. Elk

There's a mist over the bay

I'm rowing so smoothly

Where am I and where am I going

I glimpse a creature

am I right or wrong

an elk that is swimming

can show the way

I follow it so cautiously

36. Often

The opposite of opposites

is it you and me

You are of porcelain

I'm of barbed wire

You play with the children

I give them smacks on their bottoms

When I want to

you have your period

But when we both want to

then fountains flash

and fire-works

brighten up the night

But it's not too often

Crisis as usual.

37. Police

A glance

out in space

the stars are twinkling

and you feel the humbleness

to be

a little human being

in the whole universe

Peace on earth

is what you want

but in the universe

there is no police.

38. Rome

All roads lead to Rome

you have forgotten that

You think that happiness

is here

with a wreck of a man

always with a drink

within reach

Rome my dear

is where you're going

in order to start living.

39. Flag

Do I have a choice

to kill or to be killed

If I choose peace

what will you do then

Do you choose to love

or to be neutral

You are not going to shoot, I hope

if I show a white flag.

40. Teddy bear

The lions hunted me at night

I huddled up

with my teddy bear

kissed him

on his big ear

thought about tomorrow

and its little secrets

I smiled and shut my eyes.

41. Stallion

She smiled

and I fall

as always

when some female

opens up

and wants to get layed

by a real man

A stallion

that's me.

42. Morning

One morning

this wonderful week

you were gone

I was fumbling in vain

beside me

in the bed

The pit after you

was not there

The memory came back

you were somewhere else

43. Thighs

Our eyes

meet each others

Yours are brown

deep and friendly

Mine are staring and blue

But our mouths

have the same smiles

we speak the same language

Soon our lips will meet

togetherness complete

I feel you groping

up my thigh

44. Destroy

A recently released rapist

sees the white flower

when he walks

towards the path

It is so innocent

in its radiance

I can destroy it

piece by piece

until nothing is left

and nobody

can do anything

It's only a flower

Now I can destroy and destroy

but I will be free

I have learned my lesson

45. Strength

The moon's glow

I can see from my window

as you from yours

We share a lot

in addition to

our memories

when you loved me

and I was so happy

I became dependant

on you

when you were not close

I was weak

But I go on fighting

for strength.

46. The apple

I have a craving

but can't follow the desire

I must keep my BMI

But the Mövenpick tempts me

can I resist

I take an apple

it soothes for a moment

I look with a greedy grin

at the ice-cream package

But I just take another apple.

47. Bird

The seagull flies into the room

more desperate and desperate

it tries to get out

It is my brother

The window is wide open

don't you see my friend

the way to freedom

You have all of heaven

as your territory

Fly bird fly

48. Soul

If you want to capture my soul

a life beyond the ordinary is needed

I want to fly high

among tops and mountains

If you want to join the trip

ambition and courage are needed

To turn your back on mediocrity

and create oneself

never looking aside.

49. You

When one loves

the soul gets big

and common sense weaker

When I see you

there is only you

I would blow-up bridges

climb mountains

if you were to suggest that

There is no law

there are no morals

There is only you.

50. Second-rate

The early bird catches the worm

but my erection is week

and when she wants more

I make breakfast

The demons have taken a siesta

but I have my imperfection

as a first class lover

Am I second-rate.

51. The moon

The sun shines on my shadow

and I get warm

The moon is flirting with me

and I flirt back

The years pass

but the flirts remain

Now also with new women

every year

But the only one who is faithful

is the moon.

52. Arrow

When a woman smiles

in that way

watch out

for behind the mask

something is hidden

Noone knows for sure

what it is

But I shall tell you

it's the expression before the attack

the attack without mercy

that wants

to stick an arrow

into your heart

Just like a man.

53. Conversation

To look into your eyes

gives me happiness

Your deep brown eyes

that hold so much warmth

A promise of a conversation

that concerns our

innermost wishes

and perhaps later

caresses in the night.

54. Sun

The sun goes behind

and I fall

I got sensitive

when you betrayed me

I believed in us

but you were playing

your own game

behind my back

When I understand

your game

you had to go

And mother sun

became my guru

55. Love

Time flies

and the reaper is blinking seductivity

But he doesn't dare

to take a step

for when I made love with

woman after woman

I'll keep

love alive

and then I am

unreachable

for the time being.

56. Cheek

The wind is howling

I enjoy

the sting

on my cheek

My black skin

as many think

is durable

But I am

like a woman

in the shadow.

57. Open up

Humour finds

its way

to the womens sex

opens her up

so she gets

receptive to

my crude charm

And that my ladies

is my true self.

58. Thought

The children sleep

I take out the moist snuff

It's time to nestle down

in between the sheets

What would be my last thought

That I am still

one day

closer to death

or that I could have

loved my family

one more time

Who knows.

59. Lido

Why do you excercise

She runaway with another

You got a night

How virile are you

Fumbling in the dark

gives noone a second act

And everyone knows

that bourgeois women

are kinky in bed

Do some push-ups

put on your white tuxedo

go down to Lido

and play the game.

60. 16

I admired your cheekbones

your beautiful brown eyes

your swanlike neck

your golden curls

your muscular legs

your flat stomach

your tempting smile

your white teeths

and your budding womanness

- but you were only 16

61. Cloud

Cloud after cloud

passes by

Woman after woman

open up

for my gentle stroke

we got goose-pimples

mine and hers

then she leaves

Cloud after cloud

passes by.

62. Winter

My soul

freezes

every winter

and your soul

warms me

every winter

Your good soul

my evil soul

is tied together

as one

which is strong

Every winter.

63. Courage

Who will cross over the bridge

it is rickety and narrow

Under runs a turbulent river

far below

Do you dare to take a step

or two

Do you have the boldness

to let go

of worn-out tracks

Ahead there is love

adventure and success

Courage is the universal measure.

64. Lead

To be chosen

to lead

the attitudes of

whole classes

breeds solidarity

to wish for others

a good life

Breeds superiority

to stand above

to be unreachable

to command

and by god's hand

the obstructor

shall fit into

mediocracy

65. Love

A tear down a cheek

arouse feelings

no longer

You are dishonest

no-one to trust

you don't care about the children

fucking behind my back

wasting your salary

Don't cry over your life

don't feel sorry for yourself

I won't forgive you

But give me a smile

allow me to live

make yourself beautiful

allow me to breathe

Give me your body

and I will feel delight.

66. One night stand

I saw you after some drinks

and you were beautiful

My charm had an effect

and you followed me home

I watched your movements

and know the woman

who aroused my senses

for a rendez-vous in bed

You were wild

you were tender

it was marvellous

But in the morning

you were just another one-night-stand

67. Look

Your look

is tender

Your smile

is hostile

What shall I believe

What shall I feel

when it's hard

to explain

I feel numb

I dare not feel

I am dead

68. Equality

A tear in your eye

a tear in my eye

Are we equals

No you are dominant

and I am weak

You take pleasure

but so do I

We are perhaps equals

in our unequality.

69. Hatred

You look is dark

when you cry

Your eyes flash

when I betray

Your forehead wrinkles

when you don't know

I love everything about you

even your hatred for me.

70. The trees

From my kitchen window

my gaze goes towards

the beautiful

treetops

in the avenue

My memories flash back

to years of my youth

when the world was unexplored

women exciting

and work enriching

with its challenges

I'm gazing outwards again

the trees are the same.

71. Shot

The danger of a shot

towards my breast

is painful

both for you

who shots

and for me

I am injured

I'm suffering

and I will die

the doctor does what he can

I'm alive

but not my soul.

72. Christmas

It's christmas

the train is rolling

I come closer

to my childhood home

My memories rewind quickly

the winter of 58

perhaps my first memory

as an invited guest

I was proud over my bow-tie

felt like an adult

We visited the Nilssons

they were kind

I get cookies

I was three.

73. Marriage

He doesn't do the dishes

she damns his football

When he strokes her gently

she scratches

When she strokes gently

he gets amused

When she attends a course

he feels free

When he is at a pub

she mastrubates

thinking about the neighboor

She wants children

he think it's enough with her

It is called marriage.

74. Way

To walk away

and never come back

Is it my choice

What will I do

do I sleep under the bridges

or with the hookers

Shall I be a pimp

for the cheap

What does my God say

Is he proud

up there

in heaven.

75. Stab

A stab in my heart

and I fall

What can I say

your words sting

I try to keep awake

but my strength is weak

I open my mouth

but the sound gets stuck

All is over.

76. Dreamed

Why did you take your life

when the greenness reached its peak

when the meadows whispered

come lie down beside me

when girls were lightly dressed

and you saw their naked legs

when your children called you

"beloved daddy"

and I washed your hair

But it wasn't enough

not anymore

What were you dreaming about

77. The death 2

To travel mile after mile

and never get there

To love and love

and only get coldness

To bend the bow high

and never get a chance

To live year after year

until death is breathing down your neck

It's my lot

the only one I know.

78. Lady

Slowly I dare to come out

the corners don't feel safe anymore

I want to be with you

but not to dance

Your chuckling laughter

to your comments

make you delicious

in every way

That you are beautiful

we all know

perhaps most of all yourself

But that you are a lady

without comparison

only I understand.

79. Excited

Steps in the dark

Is it you

It's an old lady from the village

I'm bending bowing

the meeting is secret

noone can know

You gave me a look

I dared to ask

you showed your ring

I asked again

you nodded yes

and told me a place

I am there now

excited and afraid.

80. Glance

A glance like Beauvoir

meets me from the nearest table

It makes me embarrassed

it pleases her to think

that I am interesting

Does she see beyond my boorishness

my attempts to be a man

Does she see how small I am

how I'm longing for confirmation

An ounce of encouragement

and I grow

soon I dare to meet

your look.

81. Bury

When the seagulls glide towards

the skies

I stand still

thinking about fleeting time

of life

We live our days

with small things

we bury ourselves

in details

When we look up

or aside

we see

our hopelessness.

82. Snow

Snow is falling

flake after flake

As my dreams

one by one

they lose their way

after meeting

an unfriendly reality

Make a new try

Do something

Go against

Fight

Because every dream is worth it.

83. Itching

When the steak is finished

and only wine is left

I feel a balance

between my stomach and brain

Come into my arms

you lovely waitress

My stomach is filled

but it's itching between my legs.

84. Italy

I open the letter

and remember

her face

when she had painted it

as a clown

She loved me

at least in words

I was a man

not a boy

She wanted to admire her man

she was an Italian woman

We cried at the airport

when we said good-bye

I almost ate myself to death

when she broke up

I hide the picture

the tears come

But even liberation.

86. East river

The moon shines over the East river

from 18:th floor

I look out

My thoughts go to

the only woman

I've ever loved

Your beauty

in the twilight

when you didn't

take the ring

I gave you

But I still have the moonlight.

86. The punishment

An hour is an eternity

when they take me

one by one

though I don't want

To play cooperative

for fear

of being beaten

perhaps killed

What have I done

Is this the punishment

for being a woman.

87. Ironlady

One step at a time

to reach your heart

A rose here

a little wiener waltz there

But you are cold

to touch your neck

I don't dare

much less think about

indecent excercises

in bed

Ironlady

88. The forest

The light from the moon

creates horrible shadows

which scar me

in the forest

The winds howling

plays a trick

that scares me

in the forest

The awful calls

from all kinds of animals

scares me

in the forest

The man with the horn

out of nowhere

drives me crazy

in the forest.

89. Sophia

A beautiful swan

from our desolate north

searched for her future in the city

Her dreams of love

caught up with her

when she met Prince charming

the real one

and not some ordinary hooligan

Lightning and thunder

Pukor and trumpets

The two became one

and came into everyone's hands.

90. Elf

The mist lies thick

on the field

it is beautiful

You wander through

and reveal yourself

for me

like an elf

or like a saint

without a halo

but with a soul.

91. Brother

A down above

your lips

give me tenderness

I want to caress

your shoulders

which play

with its muscles

You cute ear

I will kiss

I have a shooting pain

in my body

but I am your brother.

92. If 2

If night were day

and if day were night

when would we make love then

If the devil were good

and god were evil

who would I then pray to

If mother were father

and father were mother

who would I cuddle with then

If my wife were my mistress

and my mistress my wife

would I need viagra then

If I were you

and you were me

What would then happen.

93. Dance

Your hair is dancing

when you run

Is it a waltz or a slowfox

or is it

your own dance

For only you can run

as you do

barefoot and in a dress

and make your hair

flow rhytmmically

from crown to waist

Shall we dance.

94. Quake

One smaller quake

and the earth is trembling

That which never would happen

became reality

for me

and millions of others

Powerlessness knew

no boundaries

I understand my wife's fright

when she disappears

into the crowds

with our newborn son

I could do nothing

in my hotelroom

far away.

95. Memory

My days with you

were easy to count

but they were filled

with substance

I counted the frickles on your nose

you removed moss from my cardigan

after the passionate love-making

in the groves beyond the fir

Every woman gives a memory

to return back to

when the day is grey

96. Demons

They attack

my demons

while sleeping

The night becomes a nightmare

will I get through it unscathed

or with fragments

that destroy the whole day

which is an expectation

of new demons.

97. Boy

When you smile

I shut my eyes

and fantasize

you were someone else

who had done that

A woman I knew

when I was young

my friend's mother

who looked at me

with flirting eyes

and a nice smile

How I enjoyed

I had butterflies

in my young body.

98. Sly dog

Your eminent smile

reaches halfway

to becoming warm

Your icy look

hides the beauty

of your blue eyes

The mole on your cheek

shows your imperfection

Your little weak chin

reminds me about a womans

You sly dog.

99. Destiny

If our souls were to meet

we will be larger

than the universe

To extend all limits

is our destiny

To attack and conquer

that which should be ours

To die a little

every day.

100. Trivialities

The morning glimmers

through my window

the neighboor's dog wants to go

to the parc

some workers are shouting

in the background

other than that it's quiet

Shall I go back to sleep

away from the world's trivialities

which make my soul numb

Remember when you were here

the flame was always burning.

101. Jack Frost

Spring is resting in its cage

knocking on the door

But the northern wind hisses

Give me room Give me room

I'm big and strong

I want to join

whistles spring

Your time will come

encourages Jack Frost

It's only easter.

102. Smile with a tear

I dreamed about a woman

whose beauty was beyond compare

With a heart so pure

as that of a small child

She woke up feelings

and all of us

who had the gift to love

loved her

She sat on her pillar

and smiled with a tear.

The End